CHILDREN'S OBJECT LESSON SERMONS

BASED ON THE
COMMON LECTIONARY YEAR A

CHILDREN'S OBJECT LESSON SERMONS

Jim and Doris Morentz

Based on the
Common Lectionary Year A

Abingdon Press • Nashville

CHILDREN'S OBJECT LESSON SERMONS:
BASED ON THE COMMON LECTIONARY YEAR A

A Revised Edition of
Our Time Together (ISBN 0-687-29775-3)

Copyright © 1983, 1986 by Abingdon Press

Library of Congress Cataloging in Publication Data

MORENTZ, JIM.
    Children's object lesson sermons.
    1. Children's sermons.   2. Christian Education—
    Audio-visual aids.   I. Morentz, Doris, 1929–
    II. Title.
BV4315.M6269   1986   252'.53   86-7854

ISBN 0-687-06495-3

MANUFACTURED BY THE PARTHENON PRESS AT
NASHVILLE, TENNESSEE, UNITED STATES OF AMERICA

To
Jim and Deb, who taught us
everything we know about children—
especially the joys of being parents

Contents

Introduction.. 11

Suggestions and Prejudices of the Authors 13

Advent 17

   First Sunday of Advent 18

   Second Sunday of Advent 20

   Third Sunday of Advent 22

   Fourth Sunday of Advent 23

Christmas 25

   Christmas Eve/Day 26

   First Sunday After Christmas 27

   Second Sunday After Christmas 29

Epiphany 31

   Epiphany 32

   Baptism of the Lord......................................33

   Second Sunday After Epiphany 34

   Third Sunday After Epiphany 36

   Fourth Sunday After Epiphany 37

   Fifth Sunday After Epiphany 38

   Sixth Sunday After Epiphany 39

   Seventh Sunday After Epiphany 40

   Eighth Sunday After Epiphany 41

   Last Sunday After Epiphany 42

Lent 45

   First Sunday of Lent...................................... 46

   Second Sunday of Lent 48

   Third Sunday of Lent..................................... 49

   Fourth Sunday of Lent 51

   Fifth Sunday of Lent......................................53

   Passion/Palm Sunday..................................... 54

Easter 56
"Keep Looking Up".......................................59
Second Sunday of Easter 60
Third Sunday of Easter 61
Fourth Sunday of Easter 62
Fifth Sunday of Easter 63
Sixth Sunday of Easter 65
Ascension 66
Seventh Sunday of Easter 67
Pentecost (group one—nine Sundays) 69
Trinity Sunday 70
Second Sunday After Pentecost 71
Third Sunday After Pentecost 72
Fourth Sunday After Pentecost 73
Fifth Sunday After Pentecost 75
Sixth Sunday After Pentecost 76
Seventh Sunday After Pentecost 77
Eighth Sunday After Pentecost 78
Ninth Sunday After Pentecost 79
Pentecost (group two—nine Sundays) 81
Tenth Sunday After Pentecost 82
Eleventh Sunday After Pentecost 83
Twelfth Sunday After Pentecost 84
Thirteenth Sunday After Pentecost 85
Fourteenth Sunday After Pentecost 86
Fifteenth Sunday After Pentecost 88
Sixteenth Sunday After Pentecost 89
Seventeenth Sunday After Pentecost 91
Eighteenth Sunday After Pentecost 92
Pentecost (group three—ten Sundays) 95
Nineteenth Sunday After Pentecost 96
Twentieth Sunday After Pentecost 97
Twenty-first Sunday After Pentecost 98
Twenty-second Sunday After Pentecost 100

Twenty-third Sunday After Pentecost 101
Twenty-fourth Sunday After Pentecost 102
Twenty-fifth Sunday After Pentecost 103
Twenty-sixth Sunday After Pentecost 105
Twenty-seventh Sunday After Pentecost 106
Christ the King 108

Introduction

The majority of the sermons in this book consist of various series paralleling the seasons of the year. Prior to each series is an introduction that indicates the things you will need. In addition to these objects there will also appear on each Sunday a key word. This word is to be an integral part of the story. Often these words may be difficult for the children to understand. If that is true, there is a simple explanation of the word to make sure the children understand it. This is a good plan for using the proper word and educating the children, rather than speaking down to them. We hope to bring them up to a new understanding. A little education each week adds up to a lot of learning over the whole year.

Use your imagination. Put yourself into the lesson. Have fun and make it fun for the children. Remember, you may have some great ideas to improve upon what we have done; do it your way. Good luck.

Suggestions and Prejudices of the Authors

This is not an introduction in the typical sense. In reality, we sat down and came up with a few things we dislike most about children's sermons. This is a result of listening to presentations of children's sermons from border to border and coast to coast, and reading many others. In order to make this introduction a little more readable and a better learning opportunity for you, the pastor and presenter, these negatives have been turned into positives. It is hoped that you will be able to use some of them and find them helpful in your preparation.

Try to get the children up front. Invite them to come forward during a hymn, indicating that this is the time for children to present themselves in the altar area. If they come forward during the singing of a hymn there should be little interruption of the service.

Never insist that they come. If you notice children who have not come forward when the invitation is given, just let them sit. Don't embarrass them. They will eventually feel confident enough to join the others.

In all probability you have a predominant age in the group of children who come for the children's sermon. Find out what that age group is and aim your sermons at them. It is always much easier if you know the age span you are primarily talking to.

When the children come forward, make sure you arrange them in such a way that you are still facing the congregation. When you turn your back on the congregation, it is exclusionary. You do not want to ignore the congregation—you are just trying to include the children in the service.

Don't expect answers. If you continually ask questions and demand answers, you'll frighten some of the children. You will also give the extroverts too much opportunity to dominate.

If you do ask a question and receive an answer, consider it a bonus, but never plan a sermon around the necessity of getting an answer to any question.

You will notice in this book that some objects used in certain lessons are given a name. The object will be the presenter for a period of weeks so the children will begin to recognize the object as the presenter. Be sure to explain clearly what the object is and the role it will play during this period.

Get the children involved with the objects. Stand up and say, "This is Herman the Hammer. Say good morning to Herman." Let the children call out, "Good morning, Herman!" It is a great way to get them involved.

Practice the demonstrations. Many times there will be opportunities to do something a bit delicate. Do not take a chance—practice the demonstration first.

Be a ham. Your children will love it. They will also relate to it. Some of the parents may think you are overdoing it, but remember that it's the children's sermon. That is the audience you are talking to, the audience you are trying to teach. Don't be afraid to ham it up.

Big buildings lead to big lessons learned. Don't be afraid to build it up and build it up, so that when the final object illustration comes, the children are ready. They will be excited about it and waiting for it.

Some of these lessons will call for the participation of one or more of the children. Pick the children carefully. Make sure they are well rehearsed so that it becomes an excellent learning experience instead of an embarrassment.

As you are going through the lesson, observe the children's eyes, because in them you will see reflected their interest and involvement—or their boredom. They will show you how you are doing.

We are not quite certain who first started using children's sermons, but we are willing to guess it was the circuit rider who never preached at the same church twice in his life. We pity pastors who are celebrating a twenty-fifth anniversary—what difficulty they must have had in coming up with twenty-five years of new and interesting sermons. But coming up with new children's sermons each Sunday must have driven them out of their minds. We hope this book is helpful and makes your life a little easier for the year of this series.

Advent

(Four Sundays)

O ur first series is Advent. We begin with a New Year's celebration, to introduce the fact that this is the first Sunday of the church year, so it's a happy new year.

The rest of Advent is based on the theme of light, a very appropriate theme to lead up to Christmas.

Don't become spoiled by the small list of objects required—it won't always be this easy!

Objects Required

☆ noisemaker or hat for New Year's Eve party
☆ light bulb
☆ candle and matches

First Sunday of Advent

Gospel Lesson: Matthew 24:36-44
Key Word: **Watch**
Object: Noisemaker and/or New Year's Eve party
       hat

H appy new Year! (At this point, use the noise-maker—if it's a horn, blow it; if you have a hat, put it on. Then again say . . .) Happy New Year. It's sort of funny to have me wish you a happy new year today. It's not even December, so of course it cannot be New Year's Day. I guess you are wondering why the pastor is saying "Happy New Year!" We all know that the new year comes after Christmas.

Today is the First Sunday of Advent. Do you know what the First Sunday of Advent means? It means the coming of Christ into the world. That's what Advent means, and that's what we are celebrating today. That is why today is the first day of the new year in the church; because this is the beginning of the celebration of Christ's coming into the world.

Some of you may have a little brother or sister. If you do, maybe you can remember when your mommy and daddy were getting ready for your sister or brother to arrive and move into your household. I am sure you remember how they set up the crib. They bought blankets and diapers, and perhaps a high chair and a playpen. Some of these they already had, some they borrowed from neighbors, and some they bought new. All this did not suddenly happen; your mom and dad had to get ready for it. This took a lot of time.

For some of you, the baby may have moved into its own room. And for others, your new brother or sister may have moved into your room, and that made it a little bit crowded. But you've gotten along fine.

Now we are getting ready for Advent and the coming of the Christ Child. He had to move into a new room, too, but his room wasn't quite as fancy as yours. That is what we will be talking about during the four Sundays of Advent—the coming of the Christ Child.

Now let's talk about our key word. Our key word for the First Sunday of Advent is *watch*. (Hold up your wristwatch.) Not this kind of watch—not the kind that tells the time—but the kind of watch that means *keep your eyes open, don't stop looking or you'll miss something.*

I am sure many of you may have been to a Thanksgiving Day parade where you saw Santa Claus, or you may have gone to stores or a mall where they are getting all decorated for Christmas. All the people who plan on selling toys and other things for Christmas are not missing out—they are getting ready, they're watching, they are not going to let it sneak by. That is the world. We are the church, so surely if the world is getting ready for Christmas, you boys and girls and your mommies and daddies should be getting ready for Christmas too. So don't forget! Keep your eyes open, don't stop looking, don't miss anything, because you have to keep watching to see what happens on Christmas Eve. It is going to come very quickly now. So keep watching, and Happy New Year from the church as we look forward to a happy Christmas.

Second Sunday of Advent

Gospel Lesson: Matthew 3:1-12
Key Word: **Repent**
Object: Light bulb

Today is the Second Sunday of Advent, and I am going to use a word that many of you may not understand. Our word today is *repent.* That is a strange word, and I don't believe you know what it means, do you? Before I tell you what it means, I would like to tell you why we are using that particular word.

These sermons for you children will each have a key word, and each will always have an object. One of the reasons I like these sermons is that instead of using a very simple key word that is easy for little children to understand, I may choose a word that is an adult word and then explain it to you so you can understand what it means when you hear it again. By the time this year is over, you will be able to understand a whole lot of new words—grown-up words.

So today our word is *repent. Repent* means *to be sorry we did something wrong.*

During these next few weeks when you go shopping with your mom or dad, almost every place you go will be crowded. When you go shopping with your parents, they usually tell you to stay close to them. Have you ever wandered off, and all of a sudden you turned around and could not find them? They were gone. You got scared! You looked around and they were nowhere in sight. Then all of a sudden you saw your mom or dad and ran over and said, "Oh, am I glad I found you." That's what *repent* means. It means you got lost from Jesus, you got scared, and you are sorry.

One of the interesting things about getting lost is that you are not lost until you know you're lost. When you wander off from your mom and dad, and you don't notice they are out of sight, you are fine. But once you find out you are lost, then you get scared.

That's what happened in our Gospel lesson today. Many of the people to whom John the Baptist preached did not even know they were lost until they heard John the Baptist saying, "You're lost from Jesus. You are lost from the Messiah, and you don't care. Repent! Feel sorry! Be afraid! Look for him and you will find him."

(Hold up the light bulb.) See this light bulb? It is just like all the other light bulbs in this church, except that it is dark and cold. Do you know why? Right now it isn't connected to anything you can plug in. There is no current to make the bulb light up. The people that John the Baptist preached to were like that. They didn't know the Messiah had come, so they were walking around like cold, dark bulbs. And what John the Baptist was saying was, "Repent! Look, the Messiah is here."

That's what the story is telling us today. If you've lost your connection to Jesus, be sorry, be afraid. Look around for your light cord, because you know the cord is here, and the current is here, and you know how you can get plugged in again and light up your life.

Third Sunday of Advent

Gospel Lesson: Matthew 11:2-11
Key Word: **Go**
Object: Candle

Y ou remember last Sunday I told you we are going to have a key word, and it will be a big word that you might not be able to understand? Well, here I am this Sunday with a word you all can understand. This morning the key word is *go*.

I am sure you know what that word means, because if one day your mom or dad told you to do something and you didn't move fast enough, they might have said, "Go!" I'm sure you know what *go* means!

As we get closer and closer to Christmas, all the Christmas decorations are up everywhere. John the Baptist, in our Gospel lesson today, is still saying, "The Messiah has come! The Messiah has come!" A lot of people were following John the Baptist. Some of them were staying with him in a little camp out in the wilderness. They were called his disciples. When he found out that Jesus was nearby, he sent some of them to ask Jesus, "Are you the Messiah, or is there somebody else?" That was a very simple question: Just give me a yes or no—are you the Messiah?

This is one of the few times in the Bible when Jesus gets a little irritated. You remember the time he threw the money changers out of the temple because they were using the house of God for selling sacrifices to the people who came to the temple? Well, this is another time when Jesus got a little upset. He thought John the Baptist, his cousin, should have known who he was. So instead of saying, "Yes, I really am," he said, "Go tell John what you see. The blind see, the lame walk, the deaf hear, and the dead come to life." That was the only answer he gave. He meant, "Go and tell John what I have done, and then he will believe." The things we see are the easiest things to believe. So Jesus said, "Go and tell John what you have seen, and he will know."

Now we are going to take this candle (hold it up) and call it our John-the-Baptist candle. Our John-the-Baptist candle announces that the light of the world has come, but we won't light our John-the-Baptist candle. Instead, we will save it until next week, and then we will see what happens to our John-the-Baptist candle, as John continues to proclaim the Messiah's coming.

Fourth Sunday of Advent

Gospel Lesson: Matthew 1:18-25
Key Word: **Immanuel**
Objects: Candle and matches

Today I guess we should explain a little something about our key word, which is *Immanuel*. It is sort of funny, isn't it, that in the Gospel lesson we heard, "His name shall be called Immanuel," but when Jesus was born, they didn't call him Immanuel—they called him Jesus. A little earlier in the lesson, Joseph was told by the angel, "You shall call his name Jesus." But everything that happens through the whole Christmas story, and very often during Jesus' entire lifetime, is the Old Testament being fulfilled—that means *happening*—just the way the prophets of the Old Testament said it would. So here we see the Old Testament quoted: "Call his name Immanuel."

Now, why should they call him Immanuel? Because *Immanuel* means *God with us. Jesus* means *God will save.* The angel said to Joseph, "You shall call his name Jesus." And this fulfilled the Old Testament prediction, "He shall be called Immanuel, God with us." So Jesus was God coming to earth to visit and save his people. That is how it started, with just that little baby with those two big names—Jesus and Immanuel, God with us.

You see what has happened now? In this last Sunday of Advent, we no longer have John saying, "Make straight the way, the Messiah is coming." We now have the angel announcing, "Jesus will be born." So now we take our John-the-Baptist candle—remember we didn't light it—but now, with the announcement of the angel that Immanuel, God with us, is arriving in the form of that little baby, Jesus, we take the John-the-Baptist candle and light it, and it becomes the Jesus candle—the fulfillment!

Christmas

(Christmas Eve/Day and Two Sundays After)

T his series includes a sermon for Christmas Eve or Christmas Day, depending on when you have your service. The two Sundays After Christmas are included also.

Objects Required

☆ mother and small baby
☆ pair of sneakers or running shoes
☆ a sign—on one side will be printed *word* (all small letters); on the other side, *Word* (with a capital *W*)

Christmas Eve/Day

Gospel Lesson: Luke 2:1-20
Key Word: **Baby**
Object: Have a mother with a small baby come up
front and stand next to the pastor during
the children's sermon.

Well, it is finally Christmas Day (or Eve). All the malls are empty now. All the stores are starting to take down their Christmas displays, and soon they will be running their after-Christmas specials. Then we will be able to buy everything cheaper.

Christmas just sort of comes to an end on Christmas Day. Isn't that a shame? Because to us Christians, Christmas Day is only the beginning. This is the day we celebrate the birth of our Savior, which means the beginning of our lives, and the beginning, not the end, of the year.

Now that it is Christmas Day (or Eve), what do you think we could have for a key word, and what do you think our object should be? Well, I just don't know anything better than *baby*.

(Have the mother with the baby come up front and stand near the pastor. If there is no baby in the congregation, use a doll. If the baby is quiet and asleep, the pastor can say, "See how quietly our baby sleeps—just the way Jesus slept in the manger on that first Christmas Eve." If the baby happens to be gurgling or crying, the pastor can say, "See how our baby is alive and kicking and crying. I'm sure the Baby Jesus cried sometimes, too. You can cry all you want and let those lungs grow nice and strong. I'll just talk a little louder.")

I'm going to tell you boys and girls a little secret. Some people think all babies look alike; but most women can always tell the difference. I don't really know why that is. But the baby that was born in the manger in Bethlehem was certainly different. Let me tell you what happened that first Christmas.

Some shepherds were in the field nearby, and an angel came to them and said, "Jesus is born." They left their sheep because they believed, and they went down to see the new Christ Child. Weeks before that, a star had appeared. Three wise men from the East believed it was a sign of the birth of Jesus, and they left on a long journey to visit the Christ Child.

Those people, so many years ago, knew that baby was very different—different from all other babies. He came to save the world. He came as Immanuel—God with us. And so today (or tonight) we need to show the same faith the shepherds showed; we need to show the same faith the wise men showed when they said, "We will go to the manger to worship the new king." Today (or tonight) that is our job—to show our faith and say, "Surely Christ is with us."

First Sunday After Christmas

Gospel Lesson: Matthew 2:13-15, 19-23
Key Word: **Flee**
Object: Pair of sneakers or running shoes

O ur key word today is *flee*. Do you know what it means to *flee?* Let me give you a little help (hold up running shoes or sneakers). Isn't it funny, when you put on your sneakers, you just feel as if you are going to be able to run faster. You wear your sneakers when you go out to play baseball or basketball; any time you want to be able to run fast, you wear your sneakers.

And that's what *flee* means. Flee means *to run away.* Now, this is not the kind of flea that gets on your dog and makes it scratch. That's a different kind of flea. This is the kind of flee that means to run away.

I am sure a lot of you know one of those kids who is always picking on everybody. When you see him coming and you know he's going to start trouble, you flee—you run away, you head for safety. Sometimes you may run into the school, or sometimes you may run home, but you don't want to be where that big bully can catch you.

Well, that is just what Mary and Joseph did in the lesson today. Herod, the big bully, was afraid of the little Baby Jesus. He had heard that the people wanted Jesus as their king, so he sent his soldiers to find and kill Jesus. Now, God just did not want that to happen to his Son. He sent an angel to Joseph and Mary and said, "Flee! Run away, stay away until King Herod is dead." So Joseph took Mary and the Baby Jesus, and they went to Egypt. They stayed in Egypt a long time—until the bad King Herod was dead.

Why do you think God had to hide his Son? If God is able to do anything, why didn't he just protect Jesus? Well, there are two reasons. Do you remember at Christmastime when we said that Jesus sometimes made things in the Old Testament come true? This is another one of those times. The Gospel lesson today says, "Out of Egypt have I called my son."

The other reason is that Jesus needed time to grow. As a little baby, he certainly couldn't stand up against the scribes and the Pharisees and the priests. He had to grow to become a strong young man. Then he would be ready to take his stand, but for now, he had to flee.

Second Sunday After Christmas

Gospel Lesson: John 1:1-18
Key Word: **Word**
Object: A sign—on one side of the sign is printed
       word (all small letters); on the other side,
       Word (with a capital *W*)

I am certain you know by now that all the children's sermons are about the Gospel lessons. And boy! That lesson today was a tough one! Did you boys and girls have trouble following it? Well, don't feel bad. I am sure many grown-ups did, too. Now let's see if there is a way we can make this lesson more clear.

I am going to play a trick on you. I am going to fool you right in front of your eyes. I will need two children to help me (select two from the congregation).

Fine. (Give the sign to one of the children so that *word* with a small *w* is showing.) Now here we have a sign, and I want you to give me a word, any word at all. (You will probably be given words like dog, cat, house, boy, girl.) That's right. Those are all words. They are good words. And what does *word* mean? A word is a term that represents an object or an idea. That is what a word does.

Now just watch this. Here is where I am going to play the trick on you. I am going to take the sign from _____ (name child) and hand it to _____ (name other child, and turn the sign around so that *Word* with a capital *W* is showing).

Now I am going to ask again. Somebody give me a word. What does this mean? (Point at *Word*. Again, you will probably hear dog, cat, etc.) No. See, that is the trick.

When we had *word* with the little *w*, that meant dog, cat, mouse, or boy or girl. (Turn the sign back to small *word.*)

Now, here is the trick again. (Turn the sign so that *Word* shows.)*Word* with a capital *W* comes right out of our Gospel lesson. Are you ready? "And the Word became flesh." That means that Jesus is the living Word, with a capital *W*. So, if you look in the Bible, *God* always has a capital *G*, and *Jesus* always has a capital *J*. When you see *Word* with a capital *W*, that means *God*.

Here it is, boys and girls. (Turn the sign to the small *word.*) With the little *w*, this means things and ideas. (Turn the sign to *Word.*) This means God. That is what our Gospel lesson said today: "The Word became flesh." *Jesus* is the new Word for the New Testament.

Epiphany

(Eight Sundays)

T his series again has a first Sunday that is a very special day and is treated as such. The other Sundays follow.

Epiphany: a star (This sermon is for those who have a special service on Epiphany, January 6.)
First Sunday—Baptism of the Lord: a small bowl of water
Second through the Eighth Sunday After Epiphany: the theme "Tell" or "Communication"

Objects Required

☆ star
☆ water
☆ telegram
☆ newspaper
☆ Bible
☆ TV set or *TV Guide*
☆ box of candy
☆ comics page
☆ mail-order catalog

Epiphany

Gospel Lesson: Matthew 2:1-12
Key Word: **Epiphany**
Object: Star

We thought Christmas was over. Now here all of a sudden, three weeks after Christmas, we come to the Christmas story again. The Gospel lesson was about the three wise men coming to see Jesus, who was lying in a manger in a little stable in Bethlehem. Now, I thought all that happened on Christmas Eve. You remember, don't you? Some of the Christmas cards you received had a picture of the shepherds and the wise men, and it seemed as though they were all there at the same time, gathered around the manger.

Well, now here it is, written in the Bible, so it must be true, that the wise men came and brought their gifts of gold, frankincense, and myrrh—not on Christmas Eve, the night Jesus was born, but a few weeks later. I guess we all better take a look at our key word to see what *Epiphany* means.

Who knows what *Epiphany* means? Does anyone know? Well, I guess I had better tell you. And you mothers and fathers should listen, too, because you might learn something.

Epiphany with a capital *E* and *epiphany* with a small *e* mean two different things. You remember we talked about the word *word*? Remember? We held up the sign with *word* with a small *w*, and we said that names things and ideas. Then we held up the sign with *Word* with a capital *W*, and we said that means *God*.

Now we have *Epiphany,* with both a capital *E* and a small *e. Epiphany* with a capital *E* means *the twelfth day,* or twelve days after Christmas, which is January 6. January 6 is Epiphany. Now when *epiphany* has a small *e,* it means *the appearance of a god.* Do you see how they go together? Twelve days after Christmas, the appearance of a god. Now, here's the star the three wise men followed, and this is Epiphany, twelve days after Christmas, with a capital *E.* That is what Epiphany is—the appearance of God twelve days after Christmas, leading the wise men by a star to worship the Baby Jesus. That is what Epiphany is. Happy Epiphany to you all!

Baptism of the Lord
(First Sunday After Epiphany)

Gospel Lesson: Matthew 3:13-17
Key Word: **Baptized**
Object: Water

Today in the Gospel lesson, we heard about Jesus being *baptized.* Have you ever seen a baptism? We it all the time right here in our church. It is one of the most amazing things, and it happens right before your very eyes. I wonder if you have any idea what really happens?

I saw a magician the other day on television. He did some really great tricks. In one trick, he put a woman in a trunk, closed the lid, and when he opened the trunk, there was a lion cub inside. Then he closed the trunk again, and when he opened it this time, the lady was back inside. I thought that was pretty amazing, and I couldn't figure out how he did it.

Well, boys and girls, let me tell you, there has never been a magician who could perform anything like the miracle that takes place in baptism, right here in our church. See this water? This water can make you clean all over—inside your body and outside your body. It can also change your name. All this happens at the same time, and it only takes a few seconds.

When this water is placed on you in the name of God the Father, God the Son, and God the Holy Spirit, it makes you clean. It also makes your name Christian. God will say to you, "This is my child, in whom I am well pleased." That is the miracle of baptism, and that is something no magician can ever do. No matter how fancy a magician's trick is, he can never outperform God!

This First Sunday After Epiphany is all about the baptism of Jesus. Because that is so special, this children's sermon was about water. For the rest of the Season After Epiphany, we will be talking about *communication*. That is a big word that we will talk more about later.

Second Sunday After Epiphany

Gospel Lesson: John 1:29-34
Key Word: **Messiah**
Object: Telegram

For the next few weeks we are going to be talking about how to tell the story of God and Jesus. Every Sunday we will have a different object to help us understand the story a little better. There will be all sorts of different ways to tell the story, and today we are going to start by using a telegram.

For thousands of years the Jewish nation has been waiting for the Messiah. Can you imagine, for thousands of years, waiting for God to come? That is what the Jewish nation had to do, and they are still doing it. Waiting and waiting and waiting.

Remember last Sunday in the Gospel lesson we talked about the baptism of Jesus? Here today, Jesus is ready to be a minister. John the Baptist makes the announcement. He says, "I saw the Spirit descend on him and it stayed. This is the Son of God."

For the next few weeks we will be showing how we can spread the Word—the good news. (Have a child bring the telegram up to the pastor.) Great! Here is the first way we could spread the news—by telegram. Let's read it. You know, you don't see telegrams very much these days. Telegrams used to be one of the best ways to send the news, but now everybody uses the telephone, television, newspapers, and so on. But telegrams are still used, and here is one right now.

Are you ready for this? Here is the big news. This is from Andrew to his brother Simon Peter, and now, after thousands of years of waiting, it says: "We have found the Messiah, the Christ." And that is our word for today—*Messiah*. *Messiah* means *Jesus, the Christ*. We have found the Messiah after waiting all these thousands of years. That is pretty exciting news. And that is our story for today.

Third Sunday After Epiphany

Gospel Lesson: Matthew 4:12-23
Key Words: **Follow Me**
Object: Newspaper

R emember last week we had a telegram that told us the Messiah has come—that Jesus is here? Now this week, Jesus is starting his ministry. We have a newspaper to help us this week. (Have a child bring up a newspaper.)

Now, Jesus didn't have all these ways to tell the news when he was here on earth, going around preaching. The newspaper headline could say, *"Follow Me."* That is what Jesus said.

Let's play a game of Jesus and his disciples. (March around the church, picking out children and saying to them by name, "_____, follow me. _____, follow me," until you finally return to the front of the church.) That is how the news got around in the days when Jesus was preaching. He walked and talked to several men, and then he said, "Follow me." That is how Jesus picked his disciples, and that is how they followed him.

Now we have telegrams and newspapers to help us tell the story. Remember, boys and girls, Jesus did not stop calling people; he is still doing it today. Right here, right now. He is still saying to you, "Follow me."

Fourth Sunday After Epiphany

Gospel Lesson: Matthew 5:1-12
Key Word: **Listen**
Object: Bible

W e have had a telegram. We have had a newspaper. Now wait until you see what we have this week. It is a book. But not just any book—this is the Bible. Now, there are thousands and thousands of books. Some of them bring us information, and some of them are just fun to read. This is a special message and a special book. This is God's Word, right from him.

Now, do you know what our word for today is? It is *listen*. Let me tell you why you need to listen to this especially well. This Gospel lesson is not like the Ten Commandments. This doesn't say you must do this or you must not do that. This says, if you want to enjoy life, and you want to have fun, and you want to please God, then you will be humble, be kind, be gentle, be pure, be peaceful, be good, be happy.

Are you listening? I told you you would have to listen very carefully, because God is telling you that this is what you should do if you want to have a good life and love God. You can be all these things because God loves you first. That is what it says in his book, the Bible.

The Bible brings you the good news that God loves you first.

Fifth Sunday After Epiphany

Gospel Lesson: Matthew 5:13-16
Key Word: **Light**
Object: *TV Guide* or TV section of newspaper or,
    if possible, a TV set

Well, we have had a telegram, we have had a newspaper, and we have even had the Bible. Now we have television. Did you ever get all set to watch your favorite television show? You get the popcorn, you get your drink, and you are all ready, only to find out after you are all settled down that the TV set is not working.

Just so you don't think there is something wrong with you when you get angry about a broken set, let me tell you that your pastor gets angry, too. And so do your mom and dad. When you are all set to have a special treat and suddenly you find out the television set doesn't work, and your special treat isn't going to happen, or you are not going to see your football game, that's enough to make you upset.

Well, without that *light* for the picture tube, all you have is a blank piece of glass. That is really no fun. Before you get upset, let me tell you that the plug is out. OK? Let's put the plug back in; now we will turn on the set.

That is what Jesus was talking about in the Gospel for today. Turn it on. Let your light shine. Don't hide it! Hold it up high so all the kids at school can see you are one of Jesus' own children. Let your light shine. The smile on your face, the care you show for your friends, can say loud and clear, I am one of his own. I let my light shine. I'm turned on. I'm plugged in. I am going to enter the kingdom of heaven.

Sixth Sunday After Epiphany

Gospel Lesson: Matthew 5:17-26
Key Word: **Love**
Object: A box of candy

The Gospel lesson today is a very hard lesson. I think it is much easier for adults to understand than for children. For your sermon, I picked a different subject. We will talk about *love.* Jesus often talked to his disciples about love.

We have been talking all about communication in this Epiphany series. So far, we have used a telegram, a newspaper, a Bible, and a TV set. After all that, I thought I was beginning to understand what communications are, but here we are with a box of candy! (Hold up the candy box for all to see.) That has nothing to do with communication.

Jesus tells his disciples a really far-out thing. He says, "Love your enemy. If someone robs you, give him more. If he hits you, turn the other cheek, but don't hit back."

I said that is far out, and I mean far out! You just can't do that. If you did, people would walk all over you. Your friends would eat your lunch, take your bike, beat you up, and you would have a pretty unhappy life.

But Jesus is not telling us to let the world or our friends push us around. He is saying that if we love him, we must be different from most other people. When people look at Jesus' disciples, they should be able to see a difference; we are not like the rest of the people in the world.

We act as if we love, because we do love. God loved us first, so we love other people. At Christmas, at birthdays, on Valentine's Day—oh, boy! That's a big one—we often give someone we love a box of candy. That does quite a job of communicating. We give the message "I Love You" all tied up in a nice box of candy.

A box of candy surely does tell a story. It says, "I Love You."

Seventh Sunday After Epiphany

Gospel Lesson: Matthew 6:27-37
Key Word: **Anxious**
Object: Mail-order catalog

I thought the Gospel lesson last week was a tough one, but when I thought about a children's sermon for this week, I became very *anxious*. We have had a telegram, a newspaper, the Bible, television, a box of candy, and now—here is a mail-order catalog. I know you get these at your house. There seems to be no way to stop them from coming. They come every day, all year long. Some people, like me, never open them; we just toss them in the wastebasket.

But I know people who pile them up, and then when they have enough time, they read every item. They get out their pen and stamps and start sending orders for all sorts of things. They just love to use that mail-order catalog. I know a woman who buys everything out of these catalogs except her groceries, and if she could do that, I really think she would.

Let me tell you what the people who send us these catalogs hope we will do. Our word for today is *anxious*. They want us to be *anxious* to buy some of the things in this book. They want us to want an item so much we just have to order it. That is not what Jesus said in our Gospel today. He said, "Don't be anxious. You don't need all these things."

You know, though, there are some things about this book (hold up catalog) and this book (hold up Bible) that are alike. Some companies send out millions of these (hold up catalog) and hope to make some people so anxious they will buy something. This book (hold up Bible) is printed by the millions every year and given to people in the hope that it will make them *less* anxious. It can help them believe that God, who takes care of all living things, can take care of them too.

You do not have to be anxious. You have this book!

Eighth Sunday After Epiphany

Gospel Lesson: Matthew 5:38-48
Key Word: **Perfect**
Object: Page of comics

We have had a telegram, a newspaper, the Bible, television, a box of candy, a mail-order catalog, and today the comics from a newspaper. I guess most of you who can read, read the comics. If you can't read, you look at the pictures, or your mom or dad reads them to you.

The comics are really neat. You know that some are even for adults? Children love "Peanuts," and so do parents. Then there is "Doonesbury." It's right there in the comics, but it's for adults. Sometimes I can't even understand it.

When I was young, we called these funny papers. We don't do that much any more. Do you know why? Not many of them are too funny. Some are all about bad people. Some are history stories, and some are just plain bad. Then again, some are still funny.

We got so involved in the funnies, we almost forgot our word for today. It is *perfect*. What is a perfect funny paper? A comic that is funny. I like "Peanuts"—it's always funny. "Peanuts" is a perfect comic. It is supposed to be funny, and it is funny. That makes it perfect.

Jesus told us today, right at the end of the Gospel lesson, "You therefore must be perfect." What makes you perfect? When you are good, and you know what that means. (Point to the comics.) Comics must be funny. (Point to the children.) You must be good. It's just that simple.

Try to be perfect this week. The comics can carry a message. It is another way we can communicate in Jesus' modern world.

Last Sunday After Epiphany
(Transfiguration)

Gospel Lesson: Matthew 17:1-9
Key Words: **Tell** and **Communicate**
Objects: All the communication objects from previous Sundays, held by the children, who are lined up across the front of the church.

H ere you see all the things we have talked about these last few weeks. There's the telegram, the newspaper, the Bible, the TV, the comics page, the box of candy, the catalog, and this week—nothing.

This week I want to tell you what really has been happening these last several weeks. Our key words—and we have two of them today—are *tell* and *communicate*. These are two separate words, but they mean the same thing. To the young folks we say, "You must tell the story." To the older folks we might say, "You must communicate the story."

Every one of the objects we have had suggests a way of telling or communicating the story. Somebody has to start by telling the story, writing it, showing it on TV, or reporting it in newspapers. Now we come to the problem of all the stories you see or hear in these (point to the objects the children are holding).

What do you believe? Believe the witnesses, the ones who saw it happen. They will tell it with such conviction that you can believe them. Peter, James, and John saw Jesus transformed. That means he was *changed.* They heard God say, "This is my beloved Son, with whom I am well pleased."

They were the communicators. They saw it. They believed it, and they told the story with such conviction that we believe it too. You can be transformed into a communicator today. Go tell what you believe with such conviction that all the other children will believe you.

Jesus loves you. That is the story you have to tell.

Lent

The Lenten Series (seven Sundays) introduces Herman the Hammer. It is important that you believe in Herman so that he can help you establish contact with the children. Dress Herman up—face, moustache, anything you choose to make him a little more real to the children.

Here we are trying to establish Herman the Hammer as the pastor's assistant. To work with Herman, you will need about a dozen very simple objects. They are easy to obtain and to use.

Objects Required

- ☆ hammer to be called Herman the Hammer, the instructor during the entire seven-week series.
- ☆ two-by-four board, twelve inches long.
- ☆ hand-printed sign: I WHO SPEAK TO YOU AM HE.
- ☆ small tack and a place to put the tack
- ☆ nail (8-penny, which will be driven into the board about half an inch)
- ☆ blindfold
- ☆ piece of string
- ☆ pair of scissors
- ☆ small nail (4-penny)
- ☆ three quarter-inch lattice-strip boards, one to two inches wide, twelve inches long
- ☆ handful of palm fronds
- ☆ cymbal, triangle, or little bell

First Sunday of Lent

Gospel Lesson: Matthew 4:1-11
Key Word: **Firm**
Objects: Herman the Hammer
        Two-by-four board, twelve inches long

S ince this is the First Sunday of Lent, I would like to introduce you to our new assistant to the pastor. Our new assistant will be helping me teach for the six Sundays in Lent, and also for Easter.

This is Herman the Hammer. Boys and girls, say good morning to our friend Herman the Hammer.

Each Sunday Herman will have a message for you, and so will I. I would like to begin my part of the message by reminding you about the Gospel lesson for the day. Remember how the devil tried to tempt Jesus? But no matter what he offered, Jesus stood *firm* and said no.

Now it is very important for us to know exactly what the word *firm* means. The way I just used *firm* is almost as good a way to explain the word as any you can find. When you say, "I want to go out," and your mother or father says no, that is being firm. When you say, "Please, please, please may I go out?" and they say No! that is being *very* firm. In the story today, Jesus was firm when he was first tempted by the devil, and then when the devil tempted him again, he was *very* firm.

These stories in the Bible are not there just to entertain us. They are there to help us. This story says to us: When you know you have a chance to do something wrong, or someone tries to get you to do something wrong, you must remember the story of the way Jesus was tempted, the way Jesus stood firm and said no.

All through life it will be the same. There will always be little devils coming up and saying, "Oh, you can do this." You have to learn, as Jesus did, that no matter how much you are tempted to do something bad, you must be able to stand firm and say no.

Now I'd like to have Herman show us how he says no. Herman is a powerful tool when I take him in my hand. I have a board here. I am going to put this board down (on a good solid base), and I am going to hit it hard. The board will not give, and Herman will not give.

Now watch this. (Whack the board.) There, you see, that was a firm stroke by Herman, and that is what we expect of you as you grow up. Stand firm for what is right.

Thank you, Herman. Boys and girls, would you like to thank Herman?

We will be seeing Herman again next week.

Second Sunday of Lent

Gospel Lesson: John 3:1-17
Key Word: **Gave**
Objects: Herman the Hammer (Before the service, hang Herman, head down, from whatever is available near the place where the children's sermon is delivered.)
Piece of string
Pair of scissors

O ur word for today is *gave*. Does anyone know what that word means? I thought I had some good news for you today.

We have a Gospel lesson that everyone knows: "For God so loved the world that he gave . . . ." See, there's our word for today—God *gave*. That's exciting! At Christmas and on birthdays, someone *gave* you a gift. That was exciting.

This morning, you notice I didn't say, "Here's Herman. Say good morning to Herman." Herman hasn't heard the good news of God's love. Oh, my goodness, did you ever see anything sadder than poor Herman the Hammer, hanging there upside down? Herman doesn't look very excited.

I think I know what's the matter with Herman. He wants to be let go. God's good news is that he gave his Son to the world to show his love. When God gave his Son, he had to let go. If you ever gave a gift to a friend, you had to let go.

(Cut Herman down.) There, I just gave Herman his freedom. Now he can join the rest of us in understanding how much God gave, so we all can know and understand God's love.

Look what happened to Herman. He was just an old hammer, hanging at the end of a string. Now that I have cut the string, I can take a firm grip on Herman, and suddenly he has power—he can drive a nail or pound a board. He can do anything I ask him to do. Herman has the power to love God. Boys and girls, Herman did it again.

Do you want to say good-bye to Herman?

Third Sunday of Lent

Gospel Lesson: John 4:5-26
Key Word: **Proclamation**
Objects: Herman the Hammer
       Sign: I WHO SPEAK TO YOU
       AM HE.
       Small tack and a place to put the tack

H ere's our friend Herman the Hammer back again, ready to help us with the lesson today. Would you like to say good morning to Herman the Hammer? Now, before I begin, our word today is a big long one—*proclamation*. Does anybody have any idea what *proclamation* means? (Remember the original instructions—never press for an answer.)

I didn't think any of you would know, so I am going to tell you. A *proclamation* is an *announcement*. I just made a proclamation when I told you what a proclamation is.

This lesson has two things to say to us, no matter how little or how big we are.

Jesus went to a woman who was just an ordinary person, no one special. While he was talking to her he said, "I am Jesus, who has come to save the world. I am the Messiah."

The first point of the lesson is that he didn't go out and find a big crowd. He came to this one woman, standing all alone by a well in Samaria, and he said to her, "I am Jesus." That was his first proclamation to this lady. Remember that he told her, "I am Jesus." And he does that to you every day, especially in church and in Sunday school. It is a reminder that Jesus is your friend.

After he talked to the woman for a while, Jesus finally said, "I who speak to you am he." That is the second point of the lesson, and here is where we are going to need our friend and teacher Herman the Hammer. Often when you have a proclamation to make, you put it on a sign. You nail it up on the wall so everybody can see it. That day Jesus made a proclamation that even now, years later, is important and worthwhile enough to put up a sign.

Herman, would you put up our proclamation? (Tack sign to anything convenient, then step back.) Herman, you did a good job of proclamation today. Now let me read it to the boys and girls. They can use it as their verse today.

This is Jesus speaking, remember—"I who speak to you am he." This was his second proclamation to the woman at the well. Jesus is saying, "I am the Messiah. I am the one who is coming during this Lenten time." Remember the proclamation of Jesus—"I who speak to you am he."

Thank you, Herman. Would you like to say good-bye to Herman, boys and girls?

Fourth Sunday of Lent

Gospel Lesson: John 9:1-41
Key Word: **Blind**
Objects: Herman the Hammer
Two-by-four board, a foot long (same board that was used two weeks ago)
Nail (8-penny nail, which will be driven about ½ inch into the board before the service)
Blindfold

G ood morning, girls and boys. Time to say hello to our friend Herman the Hammer.

Our word for today, one you probably know, is *blind*. Just what does this mean? Good! I thought one of you would know. (Again, don't push—perhaps they will not know what the word means. Just say that to be blind is to be unable to see.)

Remember the Gospel lesson for today is about a man who was born blind. This man heard that Jesus was coming through his town, so he stood by the side of the road. When he heard the crowd shouting, he knew Jesus must be there.

He cried out, "Jesus, help me! I am blind."

Today when someone is blind, we all feel sorry for that person. We try to help as much as we possibly can. But in those days, blindness was thought to be a punishment for sin. Either the person or the person's parents had done something wrong; God was punishing them. Almost the only thing a blind person could do in those days was to become a beggar.

The blind man said to Jesus, "You can make me see." Jesus was impressed by the fact that this man believed in him, but he didn't just say, "Now you can see." Instead, he put some mud on the blind man's eyes and said, "Now go to the pool and wash the mud away." The man believed enough to go and do it. He did not think it was silly or useless. And when the man washed away the mud, he could see.

I am sure we all agree that being blind is not a very nice thing. So we are going to call on our friend Herman the Hammer. He will show us just how important it is to see. Remember, Jesus can show you the real, true light. I need a volunteer to help Herman.

Here is what we are going to do. We have a board with a nail already in it. All you have to do is take Herman the Hammer and put some of Herman's power into driving that nail into the board a little farther. It doesn't have to go all the way through, just a little bit more. Do you think you can do that? Good!

(Hand the child the hammer. Just before he or she is ready to pound the nail say, "Wait a minute." Take the blindfold and blindfold the child. Turn the child around once and then tell him to hit the nail. Obviously the child will be confused. Don't let the confusion last too long. Remove the blindfold.)

Like Jesus, I am saying, "Now you can see." All right, now that you can see again, put some power behind Herman and let Herman show you how he can drive that nail.

We are not really ready to go to work for Jesus until we can see. Herman did his job, once you could see. Thank you, Herman.

Fifth Sunday of Lent

Gospel Lesson: John 11:1-16, 17-45
Key Word: **United**
Objects: Herman the Hammer
Three boards (three pieces of lattice strip about 1 to 1⅛-inch wide and 1 foot long. One will be placed on one side of the church; the other two on the other side. Herman is to be in the middle.)
A large nail

O ur word for today is *united*. Does anyone know the meaning of *united? United* means *together*. For instance, when you come home from school, your mother meets you at the door, hugs you, and says, "Welcome home." You are united. You are back together again.

The Gospel lesson this morning was one of those long ones. Unless you listened very carefully, you probably said to yourself, "I don't think this will ever end." But it was a very interesting story because Jesus was asked to bring a dead man back to life.

Jesus went to the village where his friend had died several days before and saw the man's sisters crying. Jesus said to them, "Your brother will rise." That was hard to believe, but Jesus saw that the sisters really believed he could raise their brother from the dead. Remember, unless you believe Jesus can do it, he probably will not be able to help you. But these sisters said, "If you tell him to come back to life, he will. You can unite us. You can bring our brother back to us so we can all be together again?" Jesus said, "Yes, I can." (At this point, start to walk toward the single little board, which will be Lazarus.)

Now I am going to the grave to get Lazarus. Lazarus, come out. (Pick up the board and walk all the way across the church to the two other little boards and pick them up.) These are Lazarus' sisters. Jesus united Lazarus and his sisters, and Herman will show us how it's done. (At this point, you are back at the center of the church. Pick up Herman and the nail. Tap the nail through the boards. Hold up the three boards, which are now one.)

Jesus united Lazarus and his sisters. Herman has shown us what the power of God can do—bring people back together again.

Time to say good-bye to Herman.

Passion/Palm Sunday

Gospel Lesson: Matthew 21:1-11
Key Word: **Parade**
Objects: Herman the Hammer

> A handful of small palm fronds (Completely surround Herman with the fronds. Probably it would be best to put them all around the handle, then use a rubber band or two to secure them.)

O ur word for today is *parade*. Everybody loves a parade. I am sure you all know what a parade is. Would someone like to tell me what it is? Excellent. That's what a parade is. We all love parades.

I know you have all seen a parade. The bands march and play music. The floats go by, the people wave, and sometimes they even throw candy. It's always fun. We stand on the sidewalk and cheer and clap and say to one another that this is a wonderful parade. After it's over, we go back home and forget all about it.

That is the sort of thing that happened in the Gospel lesson today. What a parade they had in Jerusalem that day! The people of the city waved palms in the air; they spread palms on the road. They even put their coats on the road for Jesus to ride over. They called, "Hosanna to the Son of David! Blessed is he who comes in the name of the Lord! Hosanna in the highest!" What a happy day that was! When it was all over, some people wanted to make Jesus the king. But Jesus went off and refused to become king. Then the people forgot about the parade.

Say, whatever happened to our friend Herman? We haven't seen him yet today. Oh, there he is. Look at him. All dressed up for the parade. He is dressed in palms. Boys and girls, say good morning to Herman.

Herman got caught up in the spirit of the parade. He is excited about this day, Palm Sunday. You may be excited, too, but on Good Friday, when Jesus died, will you boys and girls remember what today's parade was all about? And then again on Easter Sunday, when he rose?

Let's see whether Herman is able to keep the spirit of the parade alive until next week. Let's see whether you boys and girls can keep the spirit of Palm Sunday and the joy of the parade alive until next Sunday, when we will see Herman for the last time.

Would you like to say good-bye to Happy Herman for today?

Easter

Gospel Lesson: John 20:1-18

Key Words: **Happy Easter, everyone! He is risen!**

Objects: Herman the Hammer

Cymbal, triangle, little bell, pan—anything to make noise.

W ell, boys and girls, here is our friend Herman the Hammer. Today we don't have just one word. We have quite a few, but we will come to them in just a minute.

First, I'd like to tell you how much Herman has enjoyed being with you these last seven weeks. This is Herman's last day with us. During these Sundays in Lent, we have enjoyed seeing Herman in all sorts of moods. He has been strong, and he has been blind. He has had all sorts of experiences. We hope you have enjoyed him and have been able to learn from him.

Remember last week Herman was at the parade on Palm Sunday? Now he is here on Easter. He is just as happy as he can be that Jesus is risen from the dead. Herman wants to teach us his final lesson.

Herman, are you happy today? If you are, show us. (With the hammer, hit the cymbal, pot, or bell, to make happy sounds.) Herman wants to tell you how happy he is, and since it's time for him to say good-bye, he wants to leave you with this Easter thought.

Are you ready? *Happy Easter, everyone. He is risen!* Can you all say that with Herman? Let's try it. Here we go—*Happy Easter, everyone. He is risen!* Let's do it once more—real loud, now, so everybody can hear—*HAPPY EASTER, EVERYONE. HE IS RISEN!*

Thank you, Herman. You have been a good teacher all these weeks, and I am sure the children would like to say thank you and good-bye.

All right, boys and girls, "Thank you and good-bye, Herman."

"Keep Looking Up"

(Second to Seventh Sunday of Easter)

T his series of post-Easter sermons is entitled "Keep Looking Up." A little preparation will be necessary, but once you have put the materials together, your objects will be ready for the next seven weeks.

Objects Required

☆ arrow cut from cardboard, about two feet long, hand-lettered with the words KEEP LOOKING UP.

This sign is to be placed in a prominent spot in the church and left there for the seven weeks, so that you can use it each Sunday.

☆ art pad (14 X 18, or whatever size you can find)
☆ easel (to hold the art pad)
☆ box of crayons
☆ a person with some art ability to assist you, or you may choose to do the art yourself (You may even be fortunate enough to have a child who can do these simple drawings.)

Second Sunday of Easter

Gospel Lesson: John 20:19-31
Key Word: **Believe**
Object: Rainbow

We are beginning a new series of sermons. For the next seven Sundays we will be watching an arrow as it shows us how to keep looking up, and what to look for.

Let me show you what I mean. Here is our guide (put up the arrow)—KEEP LOOKING UP. We will be following this arrow for six Sundays of Easter and for Ascension. We will come back to the arrow later. Now, let's get started.

Our key word is *believe*. Who knows what that word means? It means *to accept as true or real—to know that something is true.*

Now, in our Gospel lesson today, what happened to Thomas? The other disciples said, "Jesus was here. We saw him." But Thomas said, "I don't believe that."

That's pretty bad. After all the time Thomas had spent with Jesus, and he could say he didn't believe that!

You know, when your mom or dad or some adult tells you something, if you should say "I don't believe that," they would be upset. Your friends also don't like it when you say, "I don't believe that."

Jesus didn't like it, either. The next time he came back, Thomas was there. Jesus said, "Thomas, I'm sorry you don't believe. Now I'll prove it to you," but Thomas replied, "No, now I believe."

This is so great. When you and I sometimes have trouble believing, we can remember that Jesus forgave Thomas.

(Begin to make a rainbow on a pad.) What is one of God's signs of forgiveness? A rainbow. We have a rainbow because that was one of God's signs that he forgives us. It is a sign in the sky from God. KEEP LOOKING UP!

Third Sunday of Easter

Gospel Lesson: Luke 24:13-35
Key Words: **Eyes Opened**
Object: Stars at night

J esus had just risen from the dead. Two men were walking along the road, and another man caught up with them and said, "Hello."

Now watch this. "Their eyes were kept from recognizing him." Don't you think that is kind of strange? Why would Jesus do that? Their eyes were closed as they walked along all day, and they didn't know who he was.

Do you remember on Halloween when you and your friends get all dressed up? Sometimes when you see one of your friends you probably don't even know who it is. Then all of a sudden your friend will laugh or say something, and as soon as you hear that one little familiar thing you say, "Oh! That's Charlie" or "That's Joe." We all do things that give us away to our friends.

Jesus wasn't just trying to fool these men. He needed time to give them a message for all the disciples—and that includes you and me, too.

Jesus wanted to say, "Everything that has happened and everything that will happen is just what the Bible said would happen. There are no surprises."

(Start to draw some stars on your art pad.) Did you ever sit outside as the sun was going down? First there is brightness, and then it slowly starts to get dark. Then if you keep looking up, you will see stars beginning to appear—first a few, and then more and more, until finally all the heavens are covered with bright stars.

That is what happened to these men. Slowly they started to get a strange feeling about the man walking with them. As it got dark, they could see more and more.

When the stranger "took the bread and broke it," it was as if all the stars came out. Their *eyes opened* fully, and they knew it was Jesus. They were so excited. Now they knew for certain that he had risen. KEEP LOOKING UP!

Fourth Sunday of Easter

Gospel Lesson: John 10:1-10
Key Word: **Voice**
Object: Mountain

T he key word today is *voice*. You all know what a voice is. What is a voice? Good! Now isn't it funny that the Gospel talks about sheep and shepherds, and our key word today is *voice?*

I know you are all experts on voices. At night when you are supposed to go to sleep but you don't, your dad says, "Settle down and go to sleep." You know that voice!

If you have a pet—a cat or dog or bird—that pet knows your voice. You call and it knows you.

Let me tell you a little bit about sheep, so you will understand what Jesus was talking about. (Draw a mountain on the art pad.)

In those days there would be four or five shepherds, each with his own flock. To protect the sheep, they would all get together and build a fence. In the daytime the shepherds took the sheep up the mountain, where the thick grass grows, to eat; at night they were brought back down to the safe fenced-in place. Now, all those hundreds of sheep, belonging to all the different shepherds, would get all mixed up.

But in the morning, each shepherd would call his own sheep, and the sheep all knew their own shepherd's voice. Each one followed his own shepherd.

That is why our word today is *voice*. We have to know the voice of our Shepherd, who is Jesus. When he calls, we follow.

Today, we look to the mountain where the grass is green and thick—KEEP LOOKING UP! Follow the voice of the Shepherd, so you can have a good life too.

Fifth Sunday of Easter

Gospel Lesson: John 14:1-14
Key Word: **Authority**
Object: The sun

Wait until you hear what our key word is today! Even if you don't know what it means, you know how it works. Our word is *authority*. What is the best way for me to explain *authority?* The dictionary says it is *the power to command or act.* That doesn't help much.

OK, how about this? This will be just make-believe, because I know none of you boys and girls would ever do this. All right? Suppose you have just come home from school and your mother tells you to change your clothes before you go out to play. And then you tell her you won't.

You had better be ready to duck, because you are about to find out that your mother has the *authority* to command. You just watch her move. You may not have seen her ever move so fast!

That was just make-believe, but this is real. All of you have done something to test your mom or dad's authority. If you disobey, they might say, "Go to your room!"

That is what authority means, and you know that your mom and dad have it. So does Jesus. He says, "When you have seen me, you have seen the Father." That is the authority God gave him.

(Start to draw a big sun.) See the sun—that is like God. Remember the time we said when the sun goes down, then you can see the stars? Today it is just the opposite; when the sun is shining, it blots out everything else.

The earth would die very soon if the sun stopped shining. And people would die if God stopped shining in their lives. KEEP LOOKING UP and let the Son of God show you the way and warm up your life.

Sixth Sunday of Easter

Gospel Lesson: John 14:15-21
Key Word: **Commandments**
Object: Moon

O ur key word today is a long one—*commandments.* Can anyone tell me what that means? (You should get a close-enough answer.) I looked that word up in the dictionary to see exactly what it means. It said two things: *one of the Ten Commandments* and *an order, direction, or law.* Isn't it interesting that the dictionary can help you understand what the Bible says?

Now let me tell you what it says in the Gospel. Jesus said, "If you love me, you will keep my commandments." The dictionary says that *commandment* can mean *one of the Ten Commandments.*

Jesus gave the order. That makes it another commandment, like the Ten Commandments—not just something someone said, like "Don't hit your brother or sister." That may be the law in your house, and it's a good law, but this is *the* law.

Remember our motto, KEEP LOOKING UP! (Draw a moon on your pad.) What happens to the moon in the daytime? Good! (if you get an answer—if not . . .) It seems to fade away or sometimes disappear. It doesn't really go away—it's still there, but the sun is so bright we can't see the moon's light.

"I will not leave you." That's what Jesus promised. Sometimes it may be hard for us to see him. That's because we may have moved away, but he is still there. When our hearts and eyes get used to him again, he will be there. KEEP LOOKING UP!

Ascension

Gospel Lesson: Luke 24:46-53
Key Words: **Wind** and **Clouds**
Object: Wind and clouds

Wind and *clouds*. Those are two things we know about, don't we, boys and girls?

You have seen those dark clouds that look like big waves moving across the gray winter sky. (Draw each kind of cloud as you describe it.) The white ones usually mean a warm, pretty day. Then there are the black ones that mean a thunderstorm, or maybe even snow. Clouds have a lot to do with our lives.

Wind is another thing we know all about but don't know anything about. Did you hear what I just said? We know all about the wind, but we don't know anything about the wind.

We know what the wind does: In summer it makes us cooler, in fall it blows the leaves, in winter it piles up the snow, in spring it dries the wet ground. It must come from somewhere, but I don't know where, do you?

One day Jesus was standing with his disciples, giving them some last instructions, just like the coach before a football game. There was a gentle breeze and a beautiful blue sky. Then Jesus just went up in the air until he disappeared into a great white cloud. He was gone—back to his Father in heaven.

God uses the things of nature, such as wind, clouds, and sky, all through the Bible to help us understand him better.

White clouds, black clouds, gentle winds, strong winds—these all show us that God is here now, saying, "Here is my blessing." KEEP LOOKING UP!

Seventh Sunday of Easter

Gospel Lesson: John 17:1-11
Key Word: **One**
Object: Church steeple (very high)

T oday we have a key word we just can't miss with. Everyone must know what *one* is.

If you ever saw a football game, you saw the members of the winning team run around holding up their right index fingers and saying, "We're number one!" Let me see that number-one finger. Hold it way up high so we all can see.

Now put your hands down for a minute. I want to tell you about number one as the church means it, not like it means in sports. What is the difference, can anyone tell me?

Let me tell you, then. Hold up your fingers again, real high. Fine, that's the sports number one. Now keep them up and watch me do some magic. I am going to change those fingers from sports fingers to church fingers. Ready? Here we go. We are one! Did you get that? We are one. Hold those fingers up high.

The last line of the Gospel lesson says, "That they may be one, even as we are one." We are one with God and one with one another—we are all one.

You can put your hands down now, and let's start looking up. (Show a steeple drawn on the art pad.) See that church steeple? It looks as if it goes clear up to the sky. Do you see what it has at the top? What is it? A cross! Right!

All over our town, all over this state, all over our country, and all over this world, you will find churches with big steeples, little steeples—all with a cross at the top. That tells us we are one.

Let's see those fingers—all together now, "We are one!" Don't ever forget it. If you need a reminder, when you pass a church, just KEEP LOOKING UP!

The First Nine Sundays
After Pentecost

The twenty-eight Sundays After Pentecost are not set up in a series. To assist you in lining up the objects you will need for the sermons, we have arbitrarily divided them into three groups. Here are the first nine.

Objects Required

☆ man with his mother, wife, and son
☆ rock
☆ handful of coins
☆ sign taped to a yardstick: THE KINGDOM OF HEAVEN IS AT HAND
☆ boy with a full head of hair
☆ cup of water
☆ father and son who look alike
☆ seeds
☆ weeds

Trinity Sunday

(First Sunday After Pentecost)

Gospel Lesson: Matthew 28:16-20
Key Word: **Trinity**
Object: A man with his mother, wife, and son—all
members of your church

O ur word today is *Trinity*. Who knows what that word
means? That's a tough one.

Here is what the dictionary says: *Triple person, separate but united, composed of three persons.* Well, now that we know what the dictionary says, I think you may still be a bit confused.

Let's try this. God was in the beginning—one. (Hold up one finger.) Then he sent his Son, Jesus (two fingers). Finally, he sent his Spirit (three fingers). That is three in one—God, Jesus, and the Holy Spirit. Are you still confused? Let's try one more time.

You remember in our Gospel lesson, Jesus told his disciples to go and make all of us disciples, which means *followers of Jesus?*

We are to be baptized in the name of the Father (one finger); the Son (two fingers); and the Holy Spirit (three fingers). There we go again—one, two, three—that old triple play that is a Trinity.

Here is something you can easily understand. (Have the father come forward.) You all know Mr. So-and-so. (Have his mother come up.) This is Mrs. So-and-so, you know her, too. (Then have the son come forward.) You all know So-and-so. (Have the wife come up.) And you all know Mrs. So-and-so.

(Ask the mother) Who is this? "My son."

(Ask the wife) Who is this? "My husband."

(Ask the child) Who is this? "My father."

If this man can be a son, a father, and a husband, he is really a trinity.

We understand at last—the Holy Trinity—the three in one!

Second Sunday After Pentecost

Gospel Lesson: Matthew 7:21-29
Key Word: **Sand**
Object: Rock

O ur key word today is one you all know—*sand*. There is no need to ask whether you know what sand is. I will ask, where you have seen sand? At the beach? Good.

When workers build a house, they use sand to make the mortar or cement. There is sand in the sandbox in your back yard or playground. There is sand in the bottom of the fish tank. It's all around us. We think we know what sand is, don't we? But do we really?

Let me tell you a little about sand. It is made by water wearing away at rocks for years and years. It takes such a long time. Some rocks are not too hard. These are known as sandstone. Over many years they are ground down and finally turn to sand.

In our Gospel lesson today, God said, "Don't be foolish and build your house on sand; it will just wash away." You know when you build sand castles at the beach and the tide comes in, the beautiful little castles just collapse and disappear.

God says, "Be wise; build on a rock." (Hold up rock.) That's hard, that will last. It will not wash away. The winds blow and the rains come, but if your house is built on rock, it will still stand.

When God tells you to be good, and you listen and are good, then you are on a rock. You will stand. But if you don't listen, then you are on sand. You will get into trouble.

Listen to God. Stand on a rock.

Third Sunday After Pentecost

Gospel Lesson: Matthew 9:9-13
Key Word: **Tax**
Object: Handful of coins

D o you know what *tax* means? That is our key word for today. I am certain your mom and dad know what *tax* means.

Tax is what we pay to the government. That is where the money comes from to pay the firefighters and the police, the mayor, and the president of the United States. It is money we pay for the privilege of living in this town and in America.

In the days of Jesus, everybody hated the tax collector. We don't hate our tax collectors today. We may not like to pay taxes, but we don't hate the tax collector. Let me tell you why the tax collectors in Jesus' day were disliked so much.

The Jewish nation was controlled by Rome. It was part of the Roman Empire. One of Rome's laws was that the people who lived there had to pay taxes. The Jewish people didn't like that. They didn't want to pay taxes to Rome; they wanted to be free.

The governor of Rome picked a Jewish person who could be trusted and made him the tax collector for his city. He collected the taxes and could keep some of the money. (Show the coins.)

All the other Jews said, "You work for Rome, and you take our money. You are worse than the Romans. You are a traitor to your own people. We hate you."

In our Gospel today, Jesus walked up to a tax collector named Matthew and said, "Follow me." And Matthew did. Jesus took this hated tax collector, Matthew, and turned him into Saint Matthew—the same Matthew who wrote our Gospel lesson. He became one of the chief disciples.

Jesus is saying to you, right now (show coins again), "Forget money, don't worry about a thing. Follow me." Why don't you try it?

Fourth Sunday After Pentecost

Gospel Lesson: Matthew 9:35–10:8
Key Word: **Harassed**
Object: A sign taped to a yardstick: THE KINGDOM OF HEAVEN IS AT HAND (Have a child walk back and forth, holding the sign.)

*H*arassed is our word for today. That is a tough one. It means *to bother by repeated attacks,* or *to worry or scare.*

The Roman soldiers had great power over the Jewish people. The people were always afraid of them. If you were a Jew walking down the road and a Roman soldier was going the same way, he could just say to you, "Carry my packages." The law said you had to do this for just one mile. The Jewish people didn't like that at all.

They were frightened and mistreated every day. They were *harassed*. They were so upset by the Roman soldiers' threats and bullying that they were just nervous wrecks. I am certain we would not like to have to live that way.

Jesus could tell that the people were very, very upset. He called his disciples and said, "These things just have to stop. There are only twelve of you, so don't try to go everywhere at once—start with the Jews. Go tell them the good news."

Do you see what that sign says?—THE KINGDOM OF HEAVEN IS AT HAND. That was the message those poor harassed people needed to hear. So the disciples went out and started telling the good news. Now, two thousand years later, the message has not changed one little bit.

You still have to take your sign into all parts of the world that do not know Jesus and say, "The kingdom of heaven is at hand."

No one can harass or bother you. You don't have to be afraid. Jesus is here to help you.

Fifth Sunday After Pentecost

Gospel Lesson: Matthew 10:24-33
Key Word: **Above**
Object: Hair (Have a boy with a full head of hair available.)

O ur key word today is *above*. Someone must know what that means.

Above means *over*, or *in a higher place*. For example, if you are upstairs in your room and your mom is down in the kitchen, you are *above* your mom.

When you move to a new class at school at the end of the year, you are one grade *above* last year's grade.

In our Gospel today, Jesus tells us two stories. First, a disciple is not above the teacher. You can be like your teacher, and that's enough.

I know when I was in school, and also in church school, I always wanted to be like my teacher. I hope you all want to be like your teachers.

Just remember, we want to be like, not above, the people in our life whom we love and respect—parents, teachers, friends, and so many more.

(Have the child with the full head of hair come up front and ask the following.) How many hairs do you have on your head? You don't know how many hairs you have on your head? Why, it's your head, didn't you ever count them?

You know what? I know why you don't know. You are young. You just never thought to count them. I bet your mother will know the exact number. Let's ask her. "Mother, do you know how many hairs are on your child's head?"

You know, I think my grandfather may have known how many he had. He was bald, and he may have been able to count them.

Do you know who knows how many hairs you have on your head? That's right, God knows. He cares for us, and each one of us is precious in his sight. The Gospel says, "Even the hairs of your head are all numbered." That is why God is God. He knows each of us by name. He cares for each one of us.

He will be with us every time we need him. He cares.

Sixth Sunday After Pentecost

Gospel Lesson: Matthew 10:34-42
Key Word: **Righteous**
Object: Cup of water

Here is a word that sounds kind of hard, but when we think about it, it is really a simple word we all know. The word is *righteous*. Do you know what that means? It means *doing right*.

We all know what *doing right* means. When we do something well, our parents or teachers say, "That was very good." That is doing right.

In the Gospel it says that good people should help good people. We Christians should love one another. It should show in the way we treat one another. When we see another person do something well, we should go out of our way to encourage that person. We are to be kind.

Jesus said that even giving a cup of cool water was righteous. (Hold up the cup of water.) Now, that doesn't sound like very much. You must remember, however, that the Holy Land where Jesus was teaching was a very dry country, and water was often very scarce. Even more scarce was cool water. This meant it had been drawn from a deep well and was stored in a clay jar in the shade for very special occasions.

If you shared your cool water with a friend, that was nice. If you shared your cool water with a stranger, you were doing something special, something *righteous*. The righteous person gets a reward, and the person who shares a cup of cool water gets a reward.

So we who are disciples of Jesus—those of us who believe in Jesus—must look out for one another because we care about one another. Why? Because he cared for us first.

Seventh Sunday After Pentecost

Gospel Lesson: Matthew 11:25-30
Key Word: **Yoke**
Object: Father and son who look alike

H ere is a word that comes from long ago, and you don't hear it much anymore. It is the word *yoke*.

A *yoke* is a wooden frame that fits on two oxen. (A picture may help.) There are two humps and two slings. You put one ox in each side, then hook them to a wagon, and off you go—very slowly. Oxen move very slowly, you know, but off you go.

A yoke is for two oxen. Never one, always two. So, in our Gospel for today when Jesus says, "Take my yoke upon you," it means it takes two. Jesus is willing to be in the yoke with you. Are you willing to share his yoke? You will have to pull your share of the load, but with Jesus as your partner, it will always be easy.

Some people have trouble trying to understand how it is that if you see Jesus, you also see the Father. (Bring the father and son up front.)

Let me show you how this can happen. Here is Mr. So-and-so and his son. I think they look so much alike that if Mr. So-and-so told us this was not his son, we wouldn't believe him.

We have seen how you can know the father by knowing the son. We have also seen that Jesus shows his love and concern for you by being willing to join you in the yoke. And so we see God as a loving, concerned Father.

Eighth Sunday After Pentecost

Gospel Lesson: Matthew 13:1-9, 18-23
Key Word: **Soil**
Object: Seeds

O ur word today is an easy one, one we all know. It is *soil*. Sometimes we call it *dirt*, and we all know what dirt is. I know you all go out and build roads in the dirt and race your cars and trucks all around in the dirt.

In the Gospel lesson today, Jesus is thinking about dirt. It is really called *soil*. That's what we will call it today. What Jesus is talking about is the soil where seeds are planted. He is talking about what kind of soil it is and how deep it is.

Here are some seeds. You all have seen seeds. Sometimes we plant flower seeds, and we get beautiful flowers. I think daisies are very pretty. Sometimes we plant vegetable seeds, and then we get corn or tomatoes or lettuce. Many, many vegetables are grown from seeds. What is your favorite vegetable?

Now when we plant this seed, it doesn't make any difference whether it is a flower or a vegetable. This seed will grow only if it has good soil and enough water and sun. If it has all these, you will have a beautiful garden: soil, seeds, water, and sun. That is what Jesus is telling us in the story today.

You young people must never stop working on your growth as Christians. If you stop growing, you will die as a child of God. I am talking to the children now, but you adults should listen too.

When Jesus says, "He who has ears, let him hear," he means you—all of you—big and little.

Ninth Sunday After Pentecost

Gospel Lesson: Matthew 13:24-30, 36-43
Key Word: **Enemy**
Objects: Weeds

What is an *enemy?* A person who hates or tries to harm another is called an *enemy.*

I hope you children do not have any enemies. I know you may like some people more than you like others. I have some best friends, and some friends that are not as close; but I try not to have any enemies.

Just imagine if you had people who were your enemies, who hated you and wanted to harm you. That would surely scare you a little.

Jesus had a lot of enemies when he was on this earth. They hated him because they were afraid of him. They were bad people. They couldn't understand Jesus' talk about loving one another.

In the Gospel today, Jesus shows us what enemies can do. There was a good man who went out to plant wheat. He was very careful. He put the wheat seeds in good soil. He took very good care of it. He was hoping to have a good harvest of wheat.

Now, this man had enemies who didn't want him to have a good harvest. In the middle of the night, they crept into his fields and threw weed seeds in with the grain seeds—a whole lot of weed seeds.

When you cut wheat you expect a few weeds. Most of the weeds, you can pull out when you see them growing in with the good wheat. But if there are too many weeds, you can't pull them all, so you just have to let them grow with the wheat. The weeds kill off a lot of the wheat, so you do not have a good harvest.

And that is just what happened. The bad men ruined the harvest for the good man.

Here is what Jesus has to say about this. (Hold up weeds.) "These weeds cannot be part of my harvest. Throw them in the fire and burn them. But the good grain, that will go in my barn and I will keep it."

Don't be my enemy, be my friend. Don't sow weeds, sow good seeds.

That is what God expects of each of us. He wants each of us to be a sower of good seeds.

The Tenth
to the Eighteenth
Sunday After Pentecost

H ere are the objects you will need for the second nine
Sundays.

Objects Required

☆ pearl
☆ bread
☆ barometer
☆ tin cup
☆ three children
☆ a cross
☆ two pieces of rope, each three feet long
☆ ten-dollar bill and a dime
☆ two boys and two dimes

Tenth Sunday After Pentecost

Gospel Lesson: Matthew 13:44-52
Key Word: **Kingdom**
Object: Pearl

Our word today is *kingdom*. That's not such a hard word. A kingdom is a country ruled by a king. If you look it up in the dictionary, that is just what you will read.

There is another definition, however. It reads, *the domain over which God rules in heaven and on earth.* That is not from the Bible—that is from the dictionary. And it is a very good explanation of what the Gospel means when we read, "The kingdom of heaven is like a treasure hidden in a field."

The kingdom of God is here for all boys and girls, every one. But it is not free. God wants us all to want to be with him in his kingdom. He wants us to be willing to give up all we have to follow him.

In the first story, a man sold all he had to buy the field that had the treasure he wanted.

In the second story, a man discovered a very valuable pearl, and he sold all he owned to buy it.

A pearl starts as a grain of sand in the shell of an oyster. If you have ever been out for a walk and gotten a stone in your shoe, you know how much that hurts. You stop, take off your shoe, and dump out the stone.

That is what the oyster tries to do. That grain of sand hurts, and the oyster coats it with carbonate of lime. The coating keeps growing until it is a pearl. If it is a perfect pearl, it is worth a lot of money. If you want it, you have to be willing to pay for it.

This is why God's kingdom is compared to a treasure or a perfect pearl. We should all be willing to give up all we have to get it.

"The domain over which God rules in heaven and on earth." That is the treasure, that is the perfect pearl. That is what we all want more than anything else in the whole world.

Eleventh Sunday After Pentecost

Gospel Lesson: Matthew 14:13-21
Key Word: **Compassion**
Object: Bread

O ur word today is really a great word for you young people to learn. It is *compassion.* You may think that it means *to feel sorry for someone,* and that is pretty close.

Let me tell you why *compassion* is such a great word. In the Gospel lesson today, the disciples said to Jesus, "It is almost dark. Send the people away to find some food in the nearby town."

I think this shows that the disciples felt sorry for all those people. The people had been with them all day and surely they were getting hungry. The disciples were good men. They didn't want to see anyone suffer or go hungry. So they took the problem to Jesus.

Remember, I said the disciples felt sorry for the people. They were not compassionate—they just felt sorry. But Jesus was immediately compassionate.

This is what compassion really means—to feel sorry *and to help.* (Show the bread.) Jesus didn't just feel sorry for the people, he helped. He gave them bread and fish. He didn't send them away.

Because Jesus showed us the way, now we—all of us, boys, girls, and parents—need to stop just feeling sorry for the poor and hungry people of the world. We must take bread and feed them. That is Christ's way.

I just love that word *compassion*. It is an action word. It makes us do something, not just sit and feel sorry for the world.

Twelfth Sunday After Pentecost

Gospel Lesson: Matthew 14:22-33
Key Word: **Fear**
Object: Barometer

Today there will be a little change from the usual way we do things. You know I often say, "Here is the word. Do you know it?" I think you will all know today's word, but you may not know our object. Let's see how we do, OK?

The key word is *fear*. We all know what that means. Some of us older people, as well as you young ones, are afraid of thunder and lightning. Some of us are afraid of the dark, and some are afraid of being alone. We all know what it is to be afraid of something, and it is no fun.

Well, now let's see about our object. Who knows what this is? (Hold up barometer.) That's great. It is a barometer. (If they don't guess, just tell them.) What does a barometer do? It tells us what the weather will be like in the next day or so.

According to our Gospel lesson for today, the disciples needed a barometer. When they set out in the boat, the weather was nice. Then a storm came up, and they were all afraid for their lives.

When we are afraid, we call on Jesus. Before the disciples had a chance to call, Jesus was there, walking on the water.

Poor old Peter. He was always so ready to show his faith. He was also very human. He had so much faith, he said, "Let me walk out to meet you." And Jesus said, "Come on." And Peter did.

But just as he got near to Jesus, his fear grew bigger than his faith, and he started to sink. Jesus saved him, but he also told Peter how disappointed he was: "Oh, man of little faith, why did you doubt?"

This is what Jesus says to you, boys and girls. You don't ever have to be afraid, if you have faith. And that applies to you parents, too.

Thirteenth Sunday After Pentecost

Gospel Lesson: Matthew 15:21-28
Key Word: **Begged**
Object: Tin cup (such as a measuring cup)

O ur key word today is *begged*. You all know what that means. It means *to ask again and again*. "Just one more piece of candy?" or "Let me play just a few more minutes?" or "One more cookie, please?" Now that's begging!

Now in the Bible, we usually think of a beggar as a person with a tin cup (hold up cup), sitting beside the road, calling out, "Help the poor!" All through the Bible there are many stories about beggars.

Today we find a woman who begged for something from Jesus, but she did not wave a tin cup. She called out, "Help me." We also see that the disciples begged something from Jesus, and they did not have cups either.

The woman begged Jesus to make her daughter well. But Jesus did not perform a miracle of healing until the woman proved her faith. He said to her, "You are not even one of us. Why should I heal your daughter?" But the woman kept begging.

Then the disciples begged for something else. They said, "Send her away, she is bothering us." But Jesus saw in this woman the proof of her faith. He said, "Your faith is so great, your daughter is healed."

Jesus didn't even know the woman, but he knew faith when he saw it. He did this to teach his disciples. And the lesson is just as true for you today. You can be a beggar with a tin cup or a beggar with faith.

Your faith can make you whole and well.

Fourteenth Sunday After Pentecost

Gospel Lesson: Matthew 16:13-20
Key Words: **Who Am I?**
Objects: Three children

For this lesson, I don't know whether to start with the word or the object. I know what I'll do! I'll do them both at the same time.

I would like to have three children, about five or six years old, come up here to help me. Fine. Now, I'll stand here, and you stand in a line next to me, facing the people in the church.

Now we are ready to start. The key words are *Who Am I?* So I will start by asking, "Who am I? I am the Reverend _____. I am pastor of this church." Then you, starting at this side, say, "Who am I?" and then you tell us. (At this point the children may need a little help. You may need to say out loud, "Hold it, I have to do some coaching." Then whisper to the child, "Say what I say: My name is_____. My mother and father are Mr. and Mrs. _____. I go to _____ school and I am in the _____ grade.")

Now this little game we just played is called Who Am I? Jesus did this with his disciples. He asked them who they thought he was. It was not a game with him, though. He wanted to know what these men, who had been with him so long, would answer. Who was Jesus?

They all had different answers. They told him what other people said about who he was. Then Jesus said, "Who do *you* say I am?"

Jesus asked his disciples that question, and he also asks us today. "Who do *you* say I am?" Can you answer with Peter, "You are the Christ"?

If you can answer that question in that way, you have learned your lesson today.

Fifteenth Sunday After Pentecost

Gospel Lesson: Matthew 16:21-28
Key Word: **Rebuke**
Object: Cross

O ur word today is *rebuke*. That means *to express disapproval*, or to put it so we all understand, *to tell someone they have done something wrong*.

Jesus is starting to prepare his disciples for the fact that he is going to Jerusalem and that he will be put on trial and crucified.

Peter was impulsive, always the first of the disciples to say or do something. And here he goes again.

As soon as Jesus said, "I will go and I will die," Peter just exploded. "God forbid, Lord! This shall never happen to you!"

And Jesus rebuked Peter sharply.

Why did he speak to Peter like that? Peter didn't say anything wrong. He was trying to show his love for Jesus. Since he was the biggest and strongest of the disciples, he was ready to fight to protect Jesus.

See, boys and girls, it is so easy to say the right thing, but it is not always easy to do the right thing. Jesus knew that Peter's words were just words. When the time came to face the cross, Jesus would be all alone.

Then he said to Peter, and to all the others, "Just words are not enough. If you are afraid to die, then you cannot follow me. If you try to save your life, you will lose it."

See this cross? (Hold up the cross.) This is what Jesus offered to his disciples that day. They heard what he said, but they did not understand.

Not until later (still holding the cross up), when they were all afraid for their own lives when they saw Jesus hanging on the cross, did they understand what he had said to them that day.

Boys and girls, and all of you who hear this, it is still the same. We still have to take up our crosses to follow him.

Sixteenth Sunday After Pentecost

Gospel Lesson: Matthew 18:15-20
Key Word: **Listen**
Object: Two pieces of rope (each three feet long)
        Scissors

O ur word today is one we all know—*listen.* For some reason, when we are small we are supposed to be good at listening. We listen in school, we listen to our parents, we listen to our minister, we listen to our friends. It just goes on and on.

When we are a little older, we don't seem to be as good at listening. In fact, some of us talk so much it seems we never listen.

In the Gospel today Jesus talks about two friends—he calls them brothers. But he doesn't mean brothers in one small private family. He means brothers in a great big family—we are all members of the family of this church. That makes us all brothers and sisters.

Now, if two friends have an argument, Jesus says to settle it right away and not let the argument grow.

Sometimes when you have a fight with your friend, you might say something like, "I'll never speak to you again!" When that happens, if you don't make up soon, you may discover your friend doesn't even miss you anymore. You may have lost a good friend, and you will be very sad.

All of us—not just children—must learn to say, "I am sorry. Let's forget about our silly argument and start over. That way we can still be friends."

Your church is just like you, because it is you, and you, and you. We are the church. If we are angry with one another, then our friendship ends. We are unhappy, and so are the people around us.

Let me show you how we should be. (Take the two pieces of rope, hold them up, and tie them together.) Here are two people. We tie them together in God's family with God's love, and now they are one. They have a fight (untie rope), and they are two again. (Cut each rope in half.) Look what happened. Now four people are split up by the fight.

Let's take this whole ball of rope. (Gather rope into your hands.) I will hold it up high and say, "I'm sorry. Let us forgive one another and get back together again." (Tie all the pieces together.) Now we are one again.

That is what God wants for us—to be brothers and sisters who listen to one another.

Seventeenth Sunday After Pentecost

Gospel Lesson: Matthew 18:21-35
Key Word: **Forgive**
Objects: A ten-dollar bill and a dime

H ow many times should we *forgive?* That is our word
for today—*forgive.*

You may have an idea what it means. It means that
even if you did something I didn't like, I don't want to get
even. It's OK. You are my friend. I understand and I
forgive you.

But just suppose someone does something really
bad—not just once, but many times. I guess you don't
mind saying "I forgive you" once, or maybe even twice,
but enough is enough! You finally get to the point where
you say, "No more. I have had it! That's enough!"

That is just what the disciples thought. In fact, they
believed the old Jewish law that said you had to forgive
seven times. They even asked Jesus if it was right to
forgive seven times.

But Jesus gave them a new law. The new law was: You
must forgive not seven times, but seventy times seven.
Now that is a lot of forgiving! Jesus then went on to tell his
disciples a story, so they could understand what he meant.

A man owed his boss ten dollars. (Hold up the
ten-dollar bill.) Now that is a lot of money. The boss said
he wanted the man to pay what he owed. The poor man
didn't have the money, and he told his boss he didn't
know whether he would ever be able to pay it back. He
begged the boss to forgive the debt—that is, to not make
him pay. The boss felt sorry for the man and told him he
would forget the money—the poor man would not have to

pay it back. The man said, "Thank you, thank you, you are so kind."

On his way home, this man who had been forgiven met a man who owed him ten cents, and he demanded that the man pay him the ten cents. (Hold up the dime.) The man said that he didn't have any money and begged for mercy. He promised to pay as soon as he could. The first man said, "I want my money now, or I'll have you put in jail."

The first poor man had not learned to forgive. So his boss said, "Just as you did not forgive, I will not forgive, and I will have *you* put in jail." Jesus wants us to forgive other people, just as he forgives us.

How many times do you have to forgive? Don't ask me, ask Jesus. He said 490 times, at least. By then, you will be pretty good at forgiving.

Eighteenth Sunday After Pentecost

Gospel Lesson: Matthew 20:1-16
Key Word: **Denarius**
Object: Two children and two dimes

A *denarius* is a small gold or silver coin worth ten copper pennies. That was the kind of money they used in Jesus' time; it was Roman money.

Now the Gospel story about the man in the vineyard is just not fair. This man has a big field full of grapes, all ripe and ready to be picked. He went out early one morning and hired some men to pick the grapes, promising to pay each one a denarius. Then three more times, later in the day, he went out and hired more men. And he paid each of them a denarius.

Now, here is where we have a problem with the story. Let me show you what I mean. I want two children who would like to earn a dime to come up. (Just as they are getting up, stop one of them. Say . . .) You can't just walk up here and get a dime that easily. I want you to walk down that side aisle, across the back, down the other side, and then come back here. (Then turn to the other child. Say . . .) I asked you if you would like to earn a dime, and here it is.

(When the first child gets back from the trip around the church, say . . .) I just gave _____ a dime, and he (or she) didn't do anything. He just came up and I gave it to him. Now, after the walk you took, _____ , how much do you think you should get? (If he says more than a dime . . .) Sounds fair to me. (If he says a dime . . .) I think maybe you understood the Gospel lesson for today.

You see, I have two dimes. They are mine. I can do whatever I want with them. I asked for two children who wanted to earn a dime. I paid each a dime. One worked for it and one didn't. The reason it's fair is that I kept my word. I paid what I said I would pay.

That is what happens to us. Some of us are bad. We say, "I'll be good when I get older. Then I'll get to heaven." Others say, "I'll be good now, then I will surely get to heaven." Jesus says, "No matter how long you work at it, it is my gift to give, and I will decide who comes to live with me. It is my dime; I'll decide who wins the prize in the end."

The Nineteenth
to the Last
Sunday After Pentecost

H ere are the objects you will need for the final ten Sundays After Pentecost.

Objects Required

☆ pitcher of water and two glasses
☆ bunch of grapes
☆ dish of candy
☆ one-dollar bill
☆ two Bibles
☆ one candle; two boxes of matches—
   one wet, one dry
☆ quarter
☆ organ or piano
☆ sign: THE END
☆ plate of cookies

Nineteenth Sunday After Pentecost

Gospel Lesson: Matthew 21:28-32
Key Word: **Will**
Object: Pitcher of water and two glasses

Our key word is *will,* and it can have many different meanings. It could be a boy's name. It could mean the way you leave your money when you die—you make a will. It could mean you intend to do something, as when you say, "My will is to do so-and-so."

The *will* we are talking about today is the *will* I use when I ask someone to do something.

A father had two sons and he said to them, "Will you do something for me?" One son said no, but he finally did it. The other son said sure, but he didn't do it at all. Jesus asked, "Which of the two sons obeyed his father?"

I would like two children to come and help me. (Have two children prepared to act out their parts as follows.)

(Give each child a glass. To one child, say . . .) I have a question for you. Will you hold this glass so I can pour some water in it? (The child says, "No, I don't think so," and turns his back.)

(To the other child, say . . .) I have a question for you. Will you hold this glass so I can pour some water in it? ("Sure," he says. As you start to pour just a very little, since it will go on the floor, he pulls the glass away. Water falls on the floor. At this point, the first child says, "I changed my mind, I'll help." He holds out his glass and you fill it.)

Which of these children do you think did what I asked? The one who said no, but then did what he was asked, or the one who said yes, then didn't do it?

What Jesus is saying in this Gospel lesson is this: Some people hear what the Bible says and they say, "I believe it," but they don't act like they believe it. Other people don't understand what the Bible says, but when they do understand, they believe it.

Boys and girls, don't just learn what Jesus is saying, but also live it. That is how you do the will of the Father.

Twentieth Sunday After Pentecost

Gospel Lesson: Matthew 21:33-43
Key Word: **Tenant**
Object: Grapes

What is a *tenant?* Does anyone know? A tenant is *a person who lives on another person's land and pays rent for living there.*

Do you think we still have tenant farmers today like the one in the lesson? We certainly do. All over this country there are people who farm like that. Some are still called sharecroppers, because they share the crop with the person who owns the land.

The man in the story today must have built a pretty nice vineyard. Then he found a good tenant, turned the place over to him, and moved far, far away.

He knew when the grapes would be ripe. (Hold up a bunch of grapes.) These surely look pretty, all ripe and ready to eat.

The man sent his servants to get his share, but when they got there, the tenant said, "The owner is a long way from here, why should I share with him? I did all the work." The servants were killed, and the tenant thought that was the end of that. But more servants showed up to get the owner's share, and they were killed too.

So far all we have talked about is a bad tenant and a beautiful bunch of grapes. But listen to what happens next. The owner of the land said, "I'll send my son. They wouldn't dare do him any harm."

Doesn't that sound a little like another story we know? Does anybody know who sent his Son? That's right. God sent his Son.

So, this whole lesson isn't about a tenant and grapes. It is about us. How do we receive Jesus when he comes to us? Do we try to send him away?

It says very clearly, "If you don't accept the Son when he comes to you, he will go to someone who *will* accept him."

These grapes help us understand, but it is God we are really talking about. Accept him now!

Twenty-first Sunday After Pentecost

Gospel Lesson: Matthew 22:1-14
Key Word: **Feast**
Object: Dish full of candy

What is a *feast?* Do you know? At least this word is easy to explain.

What happens at Thanksgiving time? All your friends or relatives get together for dinner. You have turkey, gravy, potatoes, stuffing, cranberries, pumpkin pie, fruit, and many other things. Oh, what a meal! By the time you get up from the table, you are so full you can hardly move. Well, that's a *feast!*

The lesson tells us about a king who prepared a feast for his son's wedding. After everything was ready, he invited all the guests to come and join him, but they started to make all kinds of excuses—they were too busy. This made the king very angry. Did you ever try to do something nice for a person, and it didn't turn out at all? Let me show you. Let's see, look what I have here (pick up candy dish). A nice dish of candy. Do I like candy? How about you boys and girls, do you like candy? I knew you would.

Now, I think I'll give this candy to the choir. (Let the choir members know you are going to do this and have them refuse to take any of the candy. Use excuses like: I'm on a diet, that's not the kind I like, too early in the day, not hungry, etc. These answers come one at a time as you offer the candy dish down the first row. Turn back to the children.)

All right, if you don't want it, then I'll have to give it to my friends, the children. They will like it. (Make sure the candy is small, wrapped pieces, to be eaten later. Have the children come up and take a piece of candy.) Thank you for coming to my candy feast.

Do you understand what just happened? Just as in our Gospel today, when the feast was ready, the guests were not ready. So the King, that's God, said to give it to the people who want it.

Boys and girls, you have just received a piece of candy. God has much more to offer. When he calls you, be ready. Don't let him offer your gift to anyone else. His gift is especially for you. Be ready to accept it.

Twenty-second Sunday After Pentecost

Gospel Lesson: Matthew 22:15-22
Key Word: **Entangle**
Object: A one-dollar bill (In God We Trust)

T he key word today has two meanings as it is used in the Gospel lesson. *Entangle* means *to get twisted up* and *caught.*

That's exactly what these men were trying to do to Jesus. That's what *entangle* means, and you can see that is what it means in the Gospel. The people did not ask this question to find out what Jesus thought. They just wanted to get him into trouble.

Jesus knew this, and boy, was he ready for them. (Hold up the one-dollar bill.) You can't see this too well, but your mom or dad can show you one when you get home. This is a dollar bill, and there is something printed on it—the great seal of the United States and the words "In God We Trust."

A lot of people get all mixed up about what this Gospel says. If your mother said to you, "Go out and play. Stay out as long as you want. Then when you are really tired, come in and do your homework," you would probably say, "Are you sure you mean that? It's all backward. First I should do my homework, and then go out to play."

People keep getting this lesson all mixed up and backward, so they have trouble understanding it. When you read it like this—"Give to God the things that are God's"—that's like doing your homework *before* you go out to play.

When you give to God what is God's, that means you support your church. You use some of that "In God We

Trust" and send it back to God. Then you are doing what God expects you to do. If you do all that first, then you will be a good citizen and "render unto Caesar the things that are Caesar's." That means you pay your taxes, just as all good people should.

You see, when you put your life in the right order, all the rest will turn out right. Put God first. It is as simple as that.

Twenty-third Sunday After Pentecost

Gospel Lesson: Matthew 22:34-46
Key Word: **Commandment**
Object: Two Bibles—one open at Exodus 20:1 (the Ten Commandments); the other at the Gospel lesson for the day.

C ommandment is a big word, but I think someone will know what it means. It means *an order,* or *a law,* like one of the Ten Commandments. Those are the ten laws God gave the Jewish people through Moses. They are laws to live by.

I'm going to read you the Ten Commandments for our children's sermon today. I doubt if many of you have ever heard them read straight through like this. I'm not going to read them just so you can say, "I heard them." I'm doing this so I can ask you a question when I'm finished. So listen closely. (Read the Commandments.)

Now, there is a funny thing about the laws God gave. What did each commandment say right away? They all had one thing in common. Want to take a guess? Here it is—each one says, "You shall *not.*"

Now, from the Gospel for today, I am going to read verses 37-40. See if you can find the difference between the old commandments in the Old Testament and the new commandments in the New Testament. Here we go; listen very carefully. (Read from the Bible.)

Did you hear the difference? In the Old Testament, the law says, "You shall *not."*

The New Testament—the Gospel, the good news—says you *shall* do something. What? That's right—love.

See what happened to the message after Jesus came to earth? Not just the old "Do *not,"* but the new law, "Love God, love one another."

Let's see all you boys and girls practice that new commandment this week. Love God; love one another.

Twenty-fourth Sunday After Pentecost

Gospel Lesson: Matthew 23:1-12
Key Word: **Practice**
Object: Organ or piano (This lesson must be set up in advance with your organist or pianist. Have a few bars of a familiar hymn played with discords all through it. Then have it played again perfectly.)

N ow, this word and this Gospel lesson make me very nervous. The key word is *practice,* and the lesson is about preachers and church leaders who just talk and never act. And it is about people who do good deeds and give to charity—not because people need it, but so other people can see these good things and say, "Isn't that a good person."

Boys and girls, if you ever think about being a minister, this Gospel lesson points out one of the most frightening things about it. A minister must get up Sunday after Sunday and tell people how to live—but a minister is just as human as everybody else.

You have to practice what you preach. How can I show you boys and girls what I mean by that?

I'm sure you all know that to play the piano or organ well takes a lot of practice. You can't just sit down and say, "I think I'll play the organ." First you must practice.

Suppose (Mr. or Mrs. So-and-so), our organist (or pianist) didn't practice. How would it sound? Can you show us? (Organist plays discorded music.) That was awful! You must practice!

Now are you ready to try again? (Now organist plays perfect tune.) That is perfect. We can tell you have practiced. Now you are not humbled, but exalted!

Twenty-fifth Sunday After Pentecost

Gospel Lesson: Matthew 25:1-13
Key Word: **Foolish**
Objects: Candle; two books of matches—one wet, one dry

I just know you know what the word *foolish* means, because we have all been foolish at times. It means *unwise, not too smart.* We all have done things and later said, "That wasn't too smart." That is what *foolish* means.

In our Gospel lesson, Jesus is the bridegroom and we are the maidens. Some of us are wise and some of us are foolish. We don't know just when Jesus is coming back to earth. But we must be ready.

Let me show you what I mean. I need two children who are old enough to light a match.

Here is a candle. It will represent the lamps in the story. What we are told in this lesson is what every Scout has learned: Be prepared!

At home we should have a flashlight ready, in case the lights go out. And we should have a battery-operated radio, so that if the power goes off, we can still hear the news. This means we should be prepared.

In the lesson, ten maidens were waiting for the bridegroom. When he came, five of the maidens were prepared, and five were not. Jesus said, "Those of you who are prepared, come with me."

Now here we are, all prepared. We have our candle. It has a good wick and is all set to burn when we need it. So let's light it. Here are some matches. (Hand one of the children the pack of matches that has been dipped in water.) Light the candle.

Well, we seem to have a problem. Maybe we were not as prepared as we thought we were. But let's not give up. Here are some more matches. Why don't you try it? (Hand dry matches to other child. When the child lights the candle, say . . .) You were prepared.

That is what the lesson says—"Be prepared." You never know when you might meet Jesus. Get your life ready, so that when you strike your match, it lights.

Twenty-sixth Sunday After Pentecost

Gospel Lesson: Matthew 25:14-30
Key Word: **Afraid**
Object: A quarter

H ere we come to another of those words we all know. Whether you are a child or a grown-up, you know what it is to be *afraid*.

I hope none of you children has ever seen any of those horrible ghost movies. I really don't understand why anybody watches them. They promise to scare you to death. I don't want to be scared—especially to death.

In the Gospel lesson today, the Master gave three men some talents—money—to use to earn more money.

Can you imagine if the Master—that's God—said to you, "Take this talent and use it for me," you would say, "No, I'm afraid of you"? We are to love God, not be afraid of him.

The first two men took what God gave them and said, "All right, God, thank you. We will just go to work and see what we can do for you." They did very well, and God was pleased with the way they used the talents he gave them.

But the third man was *afraid.* Have you ever been afraid, so afraid you could not even move? You were just frozen in fear? That can happen. That is what happened to that man. God hoped he could handle just the one talent, but because he was afraid, he couldn't even handle that.

I have here a quarter. Let us say that this is the one talent God gave you to invest in his kingdom. What would you do with this quarter, so that if God came back a year from now and said, "How did you use the talent I gave you?" God could be proud of you?

Put it in the offering at Sunday school?
Give it to feed the hungry around the world?
Give it to the Salvation Army?
Give it to help a missionary?
Give it to a poor person?
Give it to the Red Cross?

Whatever you do with it, if you give all you have to help God's world or his poor people, you will be doing the right thing. And God will be able to say, "You have used your talents well. I am pleased with you."

Twenty-seventh Sunday After Pentecost

Gospel Lesson: Matthew 24:1-14
Key Word: **Heed**
Object: A sign: THE END

In the Gospel lesson today, there is a word we don't use much anymore. It is an old-fashioned word that your grandmother might use, but you don't hear it often now. It is *heed.* Jesus said, "Take heed." That means *pay attention* or *notice.*

Now that is simple enough. Your teacher probably hasn't ever told you to take heed, but I am sure you may have been told, "Pay attention" or "Notice what is going on here."

Our lesson today is on a subject I know you are experts on. The subject is The End. (Hold up sign.) The other night perhaps you wanted your mother to read a story before you went to bed. She read you the story, and when it was over, she closed the book, gave a big sigh, and said, "The End."

Those words come at the end of a lot of things. Books often say it. Sometimes it is at the end of your favorite television show. It is always at the end of a movie. It says, The End.

You know there are other ways to say The End. When two friends part, they shake hands. When you are finished talking on the telephone, you say good-bye.

When you see a train go by, it does not say The End on the back; when you see the caboose, you just know it's the end.

When people run a race, there is a tape stretched across the finish line, and when the first person breaks the tape, that is the end. When a football game is over, they don't hold up a sign that says The End. They shoot off a gun.

In the lesson, Jesus tells us about all the things that will happen on earth, and then he says, "Then the end will come."

Take heed! (Hold up sign.) The end will come!

Christic the King

(Last Sunday After Pentecost)

Gospel Lesson: Matthew 25:31-46
Key Word: **Separate**
Object: Plate of cookies (placed so it can be seen
during entire talk)

O ur key word is one we older people know very well,
but you boys and girls may not hear it much.

When some of us were growing up, they used to
separate boys' Sunday school classes from girls' Sunday
school classes. And in school, we had a line for girls and a
line for boys. That's our word for today—*separate.* We no
longer try to separate things; we try to make things equal.

Let us think about *separate.* God thinks of us all as
equal in his sight, but when he comes to earth again, he
will be ready to separate his people from those who chose
not to follow him. How can we tell who is a follower and
who is not? Do you remember the lesson that showed us
that actions speak louder than words?

This is the last Sunday of the church year. Next Sunday
will be the First Sunday of Advent, and that is the
beginning of the new church year.

I think there is a real message here for you boys and
girls. As we end the church year, two Gospel lessons say,
"Don't just talk, do!"

(Pick up the plate of cookies. You may even want to
take one as if you were going to eat it.)

Oh, I'm sorry. I have these delicious cookies here, and I
almost forgot to ask if you would like one. Here, have one
(pass the plate around).

When I was hungry, you fed me. When I was thirsty, you gave me drink. When I was naked, you gave me clothes. The cookie I just gave you is a symbol of what God expects of us. Don't just talk. Do. God expects us to take care of one another. We are our brothers' and sisters' keepers. God will come someday to separate those who just talk from those who do. Speak up for Jesus. Make your actions and your life speak louder than your words.